JONNY LAMBERT'S
Bear and Bird
Winter Wonderland
Adventure

WHAT TO SPOT!

Use the "CAN YOU SPOT?" panels on every page to discover hidden winter secrets as you join Bear and Bird on their snowy adventure.

 Can you name the flower growing by Bear and Bird's cave?

CAN YOU HELP?

Can you help Bear and Bird find what they are looking for?

For everyone looking for a snowy adventure —Jonny Lambert

JONNY LAMBERT'S

Bear and Bird
Winter Wonderland
Adventure

DK

CAN YOU SPOT?

Toad

Bumblebee

Snake

As the last of the autumn leaves fell,
Bear and Bird went into the forest to find
berries and nuts to fill their winter store.

Bear shivered.
"Brrr! I'm cold. Let's forage as quickly
as we can, so we can hurry back home."

Where is
the bumpy
brown toad?

CAN YOU SPOT?

Berries

Hazelnuts

Autumn leaves

Log

"I agree," chirped Bird.
"It's cold enough to snow!"

CAN YOU SPOT?

Snow

Icicles

Reindeer

Harp seal

Snowdrop

The following morning, Bear stepped outside and gasped.

"Whoa... Bird, you were right. It's snowing!"
Icicles had formed around the cave door, and snow covered the ground as far as they could see.

Bear and Bird looked at each other excitedly. They knew that tonight, up in the mountains, they'd see something magical.

"Let's get ready!" chirped Bird.

Can you name the flower growing by Bear and Bird's cave?

Bear and Bird wrapped up warmly and set off through the deepening snow.

"Come on! We'd better hurry!" urged Bird. "We don't want to be late."

What is Bear wearing around his neck?

CAN YOU SPOT?

Scarf

Basket

Snowflake

Pine tree

"I'm coming," puffed Bear, as he trudged after Bird. "I've got our big blanket, and the basket is packed with hot drinks and tasty snacks."

CAN YOU SPOT?

Knitted hat

Sled

Earmuffs

Snowball

Snowy owl

Snowman

Bear and Bird hadn't walked very far when they heard laughter.

"Yippee, woohoo, ha, ha! Look at me!" shouted Fox.

Fox suddenly sped down a snowy bank on his bright red sled.

"Hey, do you want a snowball fight?" cried Moose.

"We can't—we're going to see something really special," replied Bear.

"Come along and join us," added Bird.

"What are you going to see?" asked Fox.

"It's a surprise. You'll have to wait and see," laughed Bear.

Who is sitting on the lantern?

CAN YOU SPOT?

Snow goose

Dam

Seeds

Polar bear

Ice

Bear led the way down a snowy bank until they reached an icy river. There they found two snow geese pecking at the snow.

"What are you looking for?" asked Bird.

"We're searching for something to eat but the snow is too deep," honked one of the geese.

Bear grabbed a handful of seeds from his basket. "Have some of our food," he smiled.

"Thank you!" honked the geese, and they happily gobbled up the seeds.

What type of bear is standing on the snowy hill?

CAN YOU SPOT?

River

Fungi

Moss

Squirrel

When their tummies were full, the geese flapped
their large black and white wings and
rose into the evening light.

"We must travel south, where it is warmer."
And honking goodbye, they disappeared.

Which green plant is growing on the log?

"See you in the spring!" called out Bear.

"We must keep going," chirped Bird,
"or we'll miss the surprise. If we go through
the forest, we'll make it there in time."

Nighttime fell as the friends
entered the dark, dense pine forest.
"This is very scary," muttered Moose.
"Do we have to go through here?"

Which insect is
flying close to
the moon?

CAN YOU SPOT?

Candle

Lantern

Moth

Moon

"Don't worry," Bear said reassuringly.
"We'll use the lantern to guide our way."

They hurried on, until Fox yelped,
"Look! Over there... creepy shadows!"

CAN YOU SPOT?

Boots

Gloves

Mistletoe

What special winter shoes is Wolf wearing?

Suddenly, Wolf cub and Beaver kit
jumped out from behind a tree.

"Did we scare you?" chuckled Wolf.

"Yes, you did!" yapped Fox.
"What are you doing here?
You should both be in bed!"

CAN YOU SPOT?

Pine needles

Pine cone

Mittens

"Well, it's too late to take you home,"
said Bird. "You'll have to come with us."

"Where are we going?" giggled Beaver. "Is it somewhere exciting?"

"You'll have to wait and see," replied Bear.

CAN YOU SPOT?

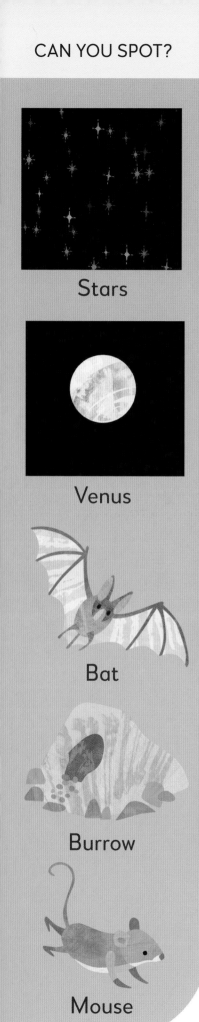

Stars

Venus

Bat

Burrow

Mouse

As they continued on with their journey,
the sky filled with twinkling stars.

"Oh, my," sighed Moose. "They are beautiful."

How many bats
can you see?

"I have never seen so many stars before," whispered Wolf.
Beaver didn't say a word. He just stared in awe.

"And if you look closely," said Fox, "you can see the planet Venus, too."

What is the name of the constellation?

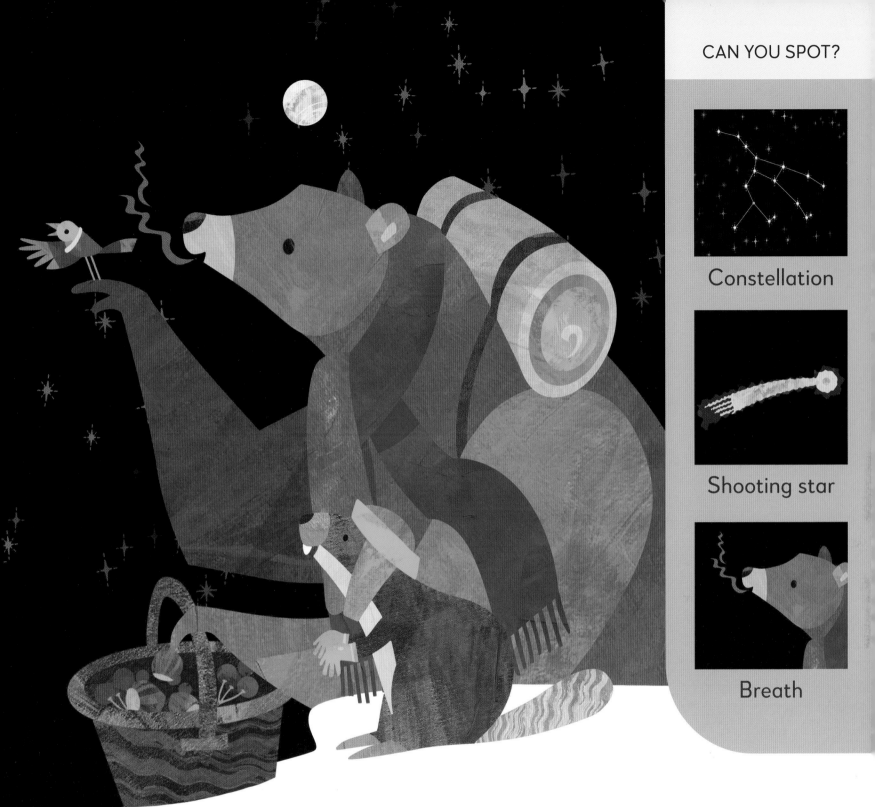

CAN YOU SPOT?

Constellation

Shooting star

Breath

"Look, Bear!" chirped Bird excitedly.
"That's your starry constellation—the Great Bear!"

Then a bright light streaked across the sky. "Oh, wow!" exclaimed Fox.
"That's the first time I've ever seen a shooting star!"

"We must go," urged Bear, "or we'll miss the big surprise."

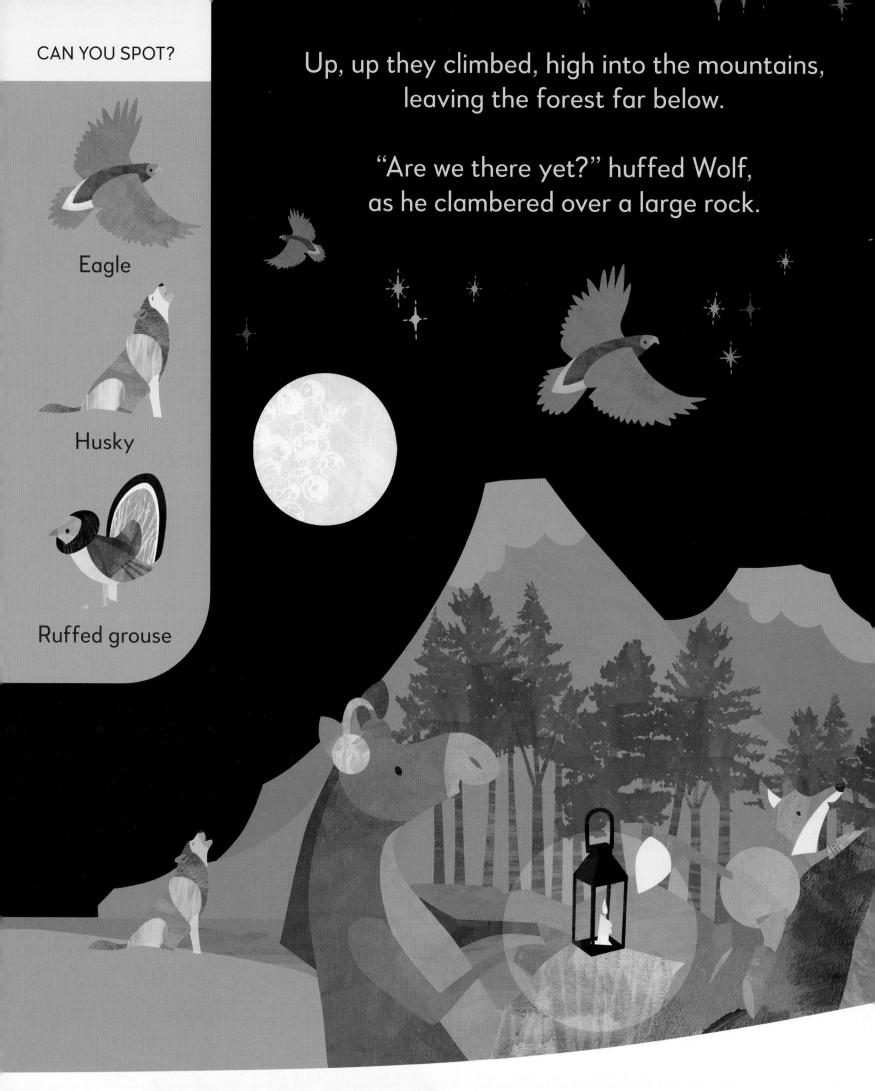

CAN YOU SPOT?

Eagle

Husky

Ruffed grouse

Up, up they climbed, high into the mountains,
leaving the forest far below.

"Are we there yet?" huffed Wolf,
as he clambered over a large rock.

Which big bird is soaring in the sky?

"We're nearly there," puffed Bear.
"It'll be worth it when we reach the top."

What sweet treat are the friends eating?

Finally, they reached the summit.
Bear laid the big blanket on the ground,
and handed out hot drinks and cookies.

"Look over there," he said quietly. "It's about to begin."

As they watched, a green glow appeared in the distance. It grew bigger, and became brighter, until...

CAN YOU SPOT?

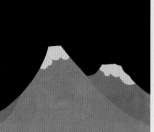

Mountains

Lake

Cookies

Blanket

The sky was filled with the
magical Northern lights!

What did we see on our winter adventure?

Snowdrop

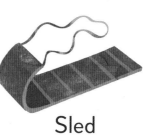
Sled

Dam

Toad

Log

Scarf

Earmuffs

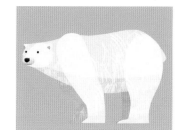
Seeds

Bumblebee

Snow

Snowball

Snake

Icicles

Basket

Snowy owl

Polar bear

Berries

Snowflake

Ice

Hazelnuts

Reindeer

Pine tree

Snowman

River

Autumn leaves

Harp seal

Knitted hat

Snow goose

Fungi

Moss

Boots

Stars

Constellation

Ruffed grouse

Squirrel

Gloves

Venus

Shooting star

Mountains

Candle

Mistletoe

Lantern

Pine needles

Bat

Breath

Lake

Moth

Pine cone

Burrow

Eagle

Cookies

Moon

Mittens

Mouse

Husky

Blanket

DK | Penguin Random House

Produced for DK by Plum 5 Ltd

Illustrated and written by Jonny Lambert
Editor Rea Pikula
Designer Eleanor Bates
US Senior Editor Shannon Beatty
Jacket Coordinator Elin Woosnam
Managing Editor Penny Smith
Art Director Mabel Chan
Production Editor Dragana Puvacic
Senior Production Controller Inderjit Bhullar
Publisher Francesca Young
Managing Director Sarah Larter

First American Edition, 2024
Published in the United States by DK Publishing,
a division of Penguin Random House LLC
1745 Broadway, 20th Floor, New York, NY 10019

A catalog record for this book
is available from the Library of Congress.
ISBN: 978–0–5938–4353–6

DK books are available at special discounts when purchased
in bulk for sales promotions, premiums, fund-raising,
or educational use.
For details, contact: DK Publishing Special Markets,
1745 Broadway, 20th Floor, New York, NY 10019
SpecialSales@dk.com

Printed and bound in China

www.dk.com